COLORING B

FUNNY ANIMALS

25 amazing illustrations

Artworks by
Alena Lazareva

www.alenalazareva.com

Happy coloring!

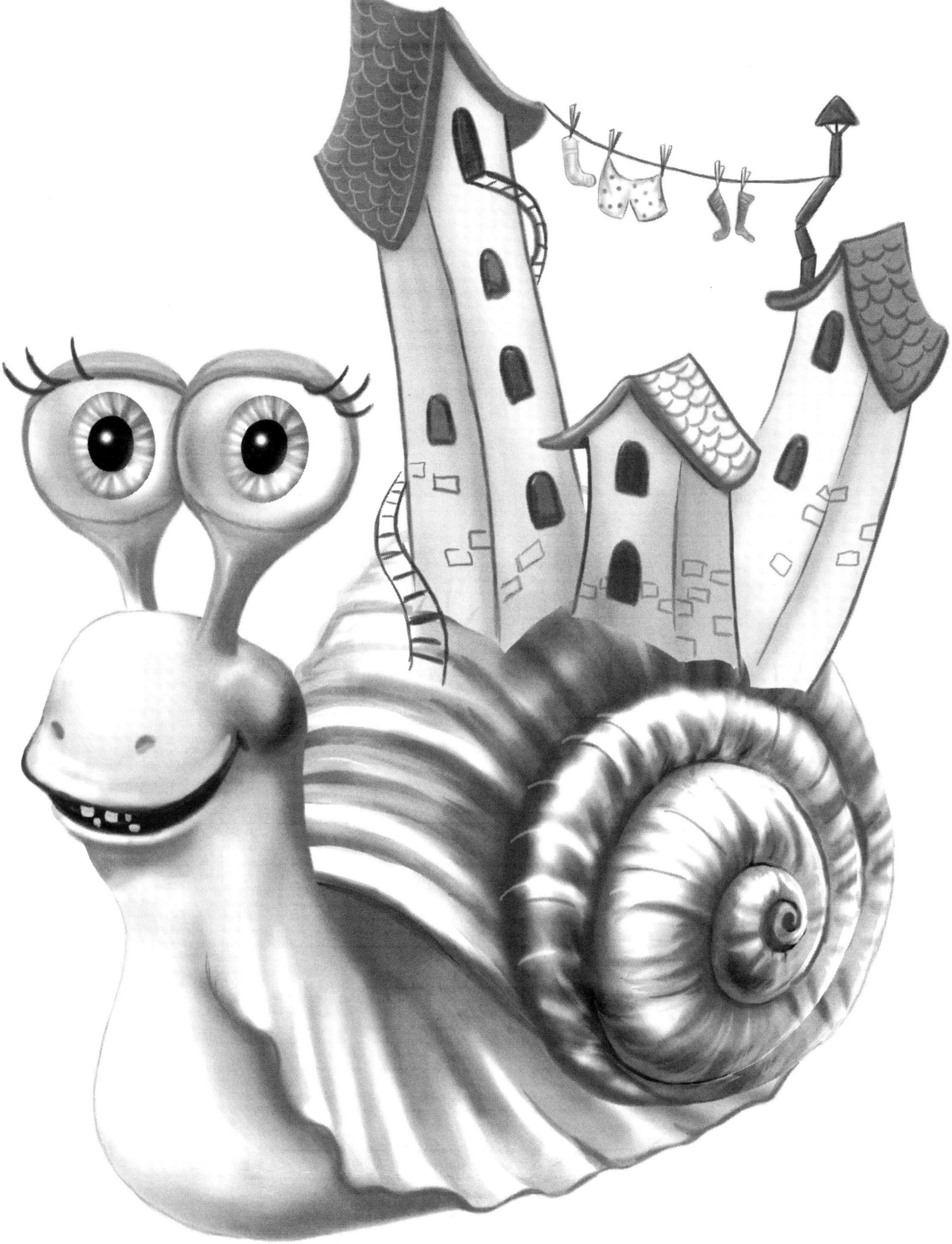

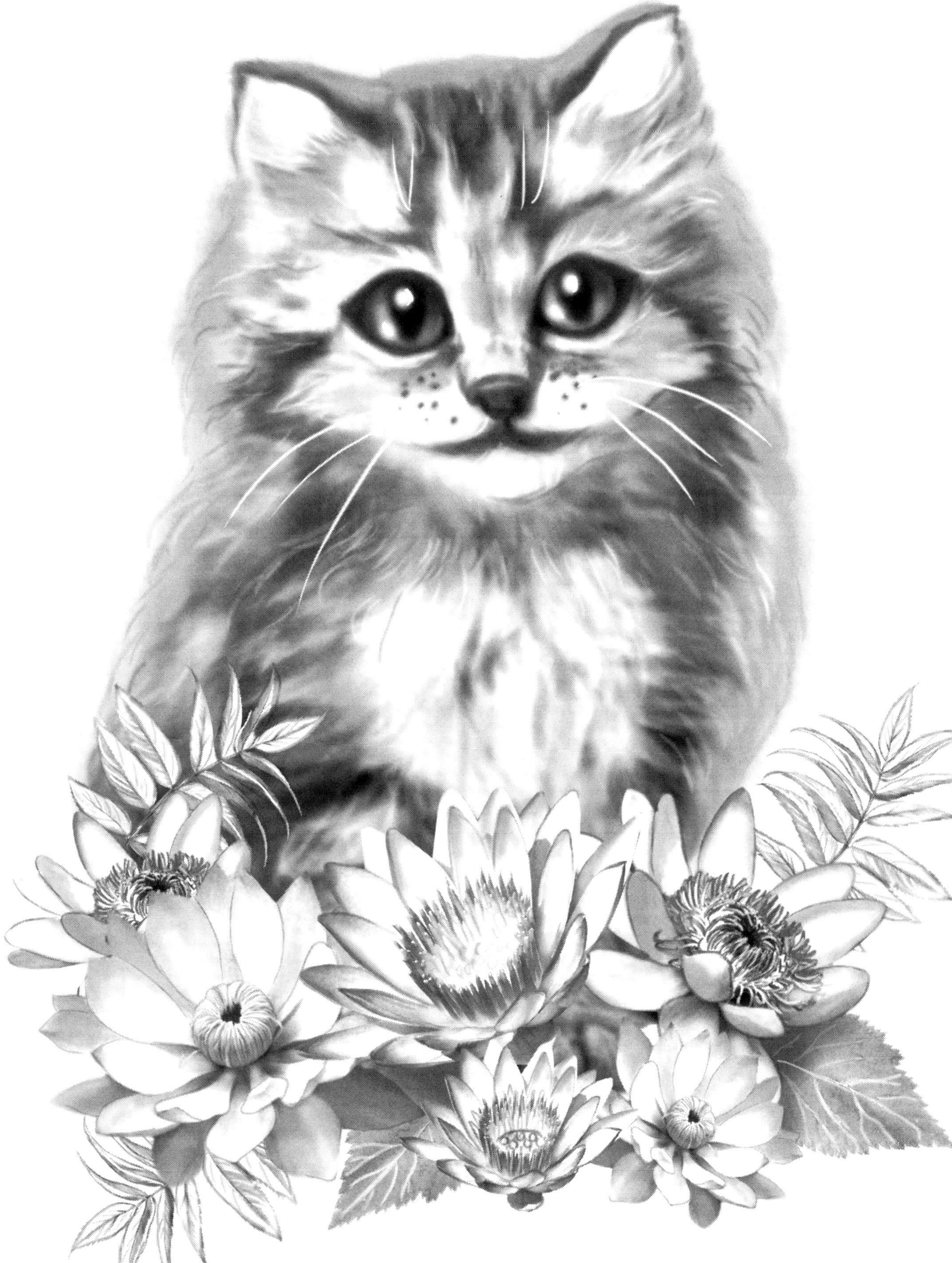

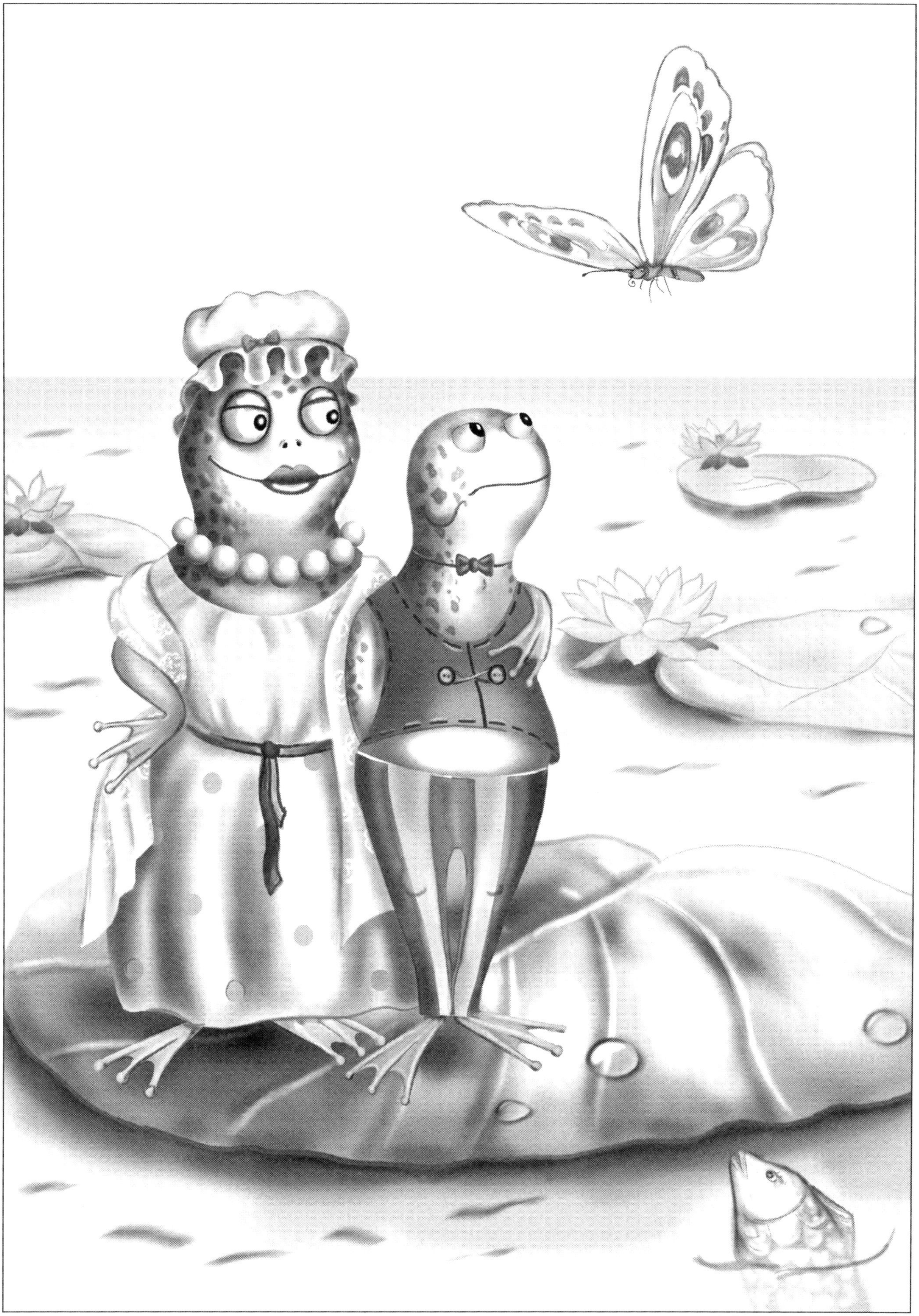

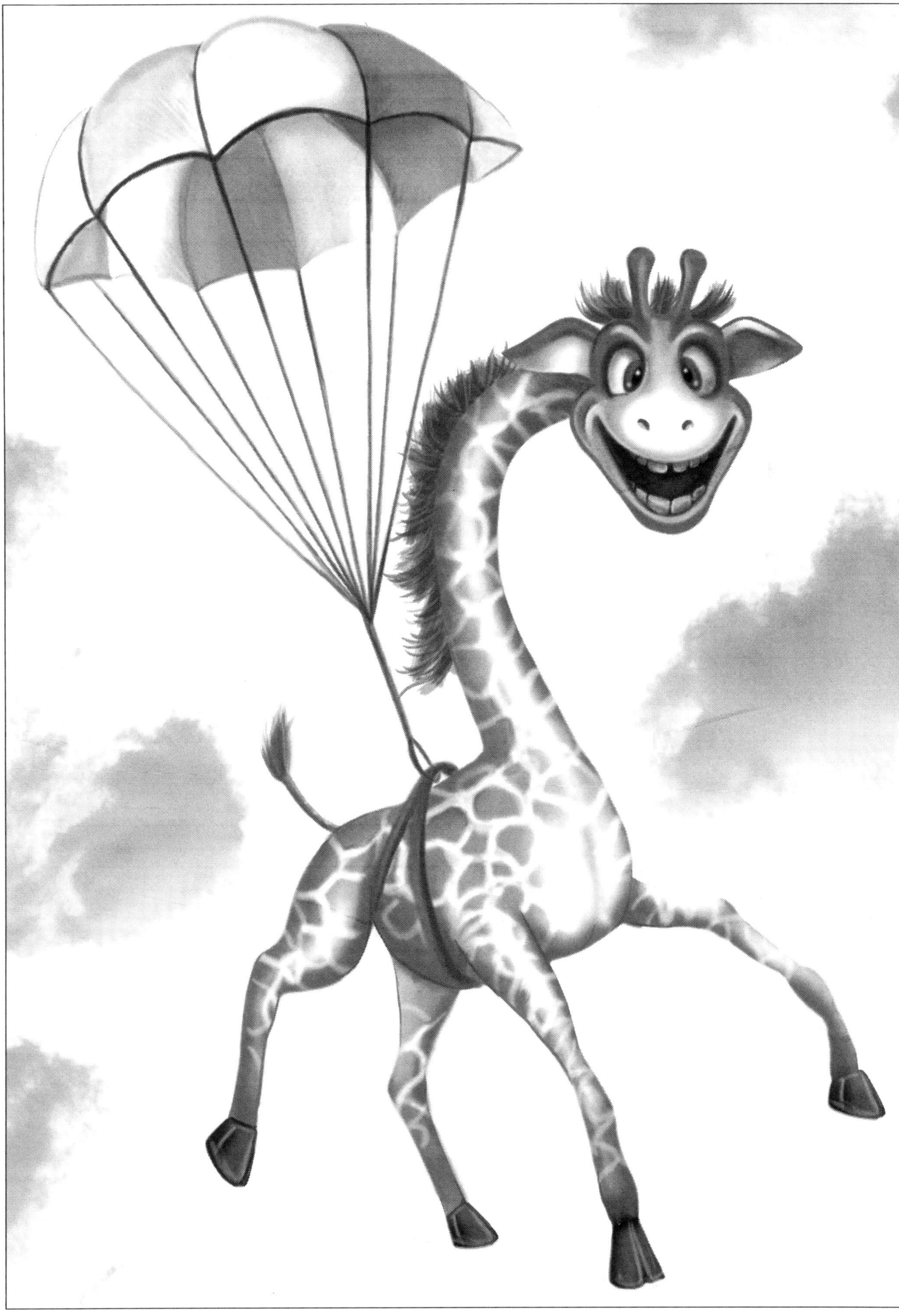

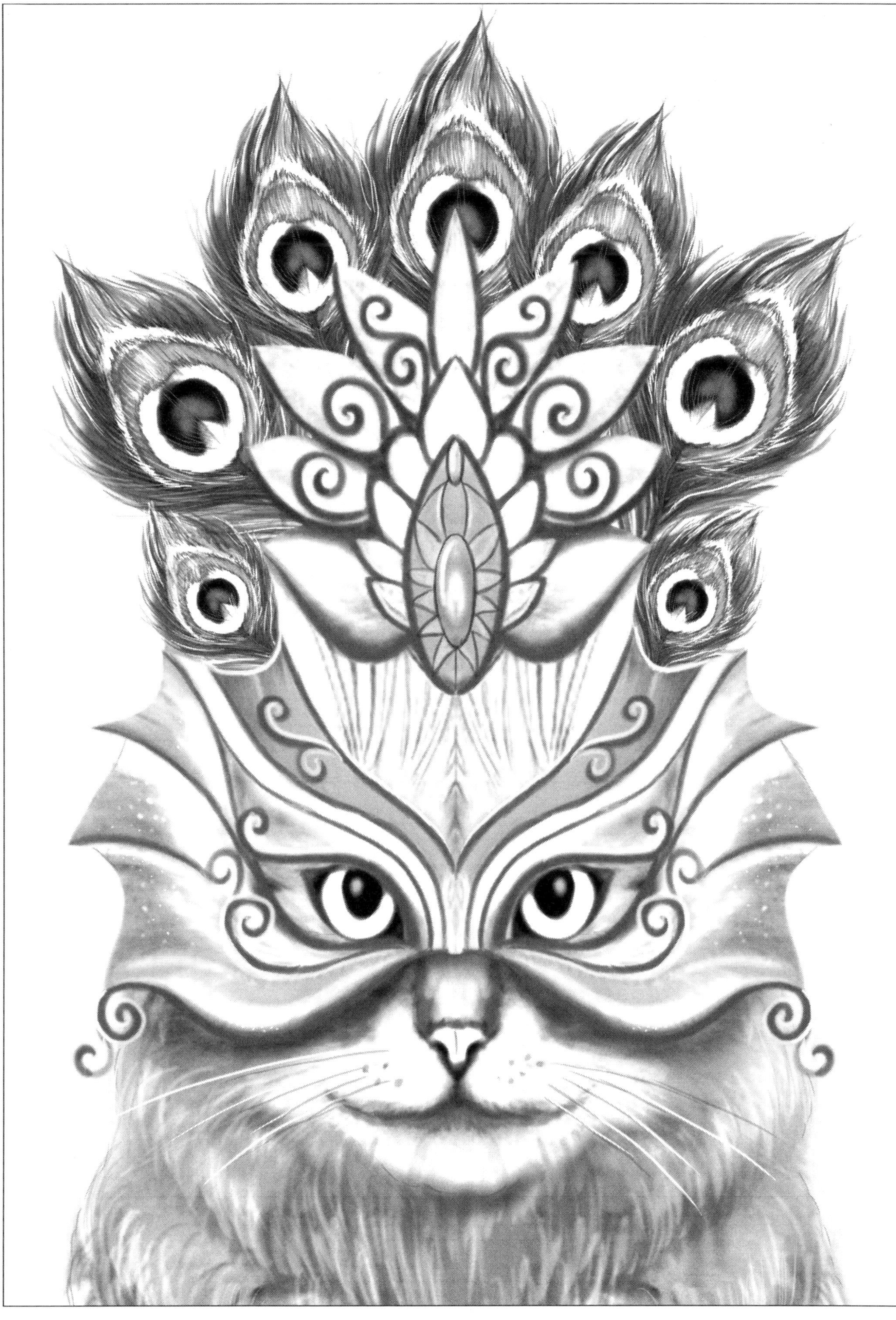

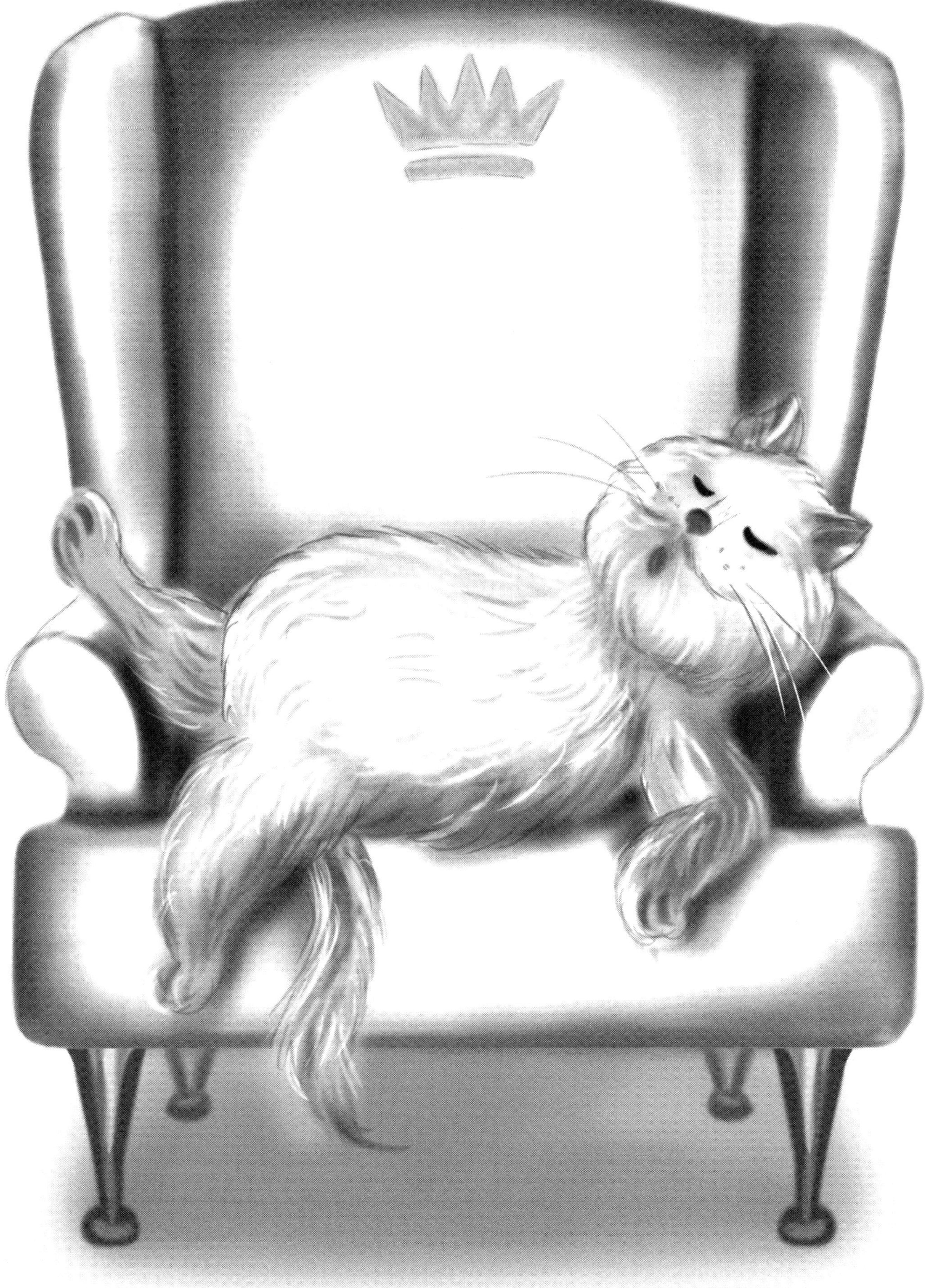

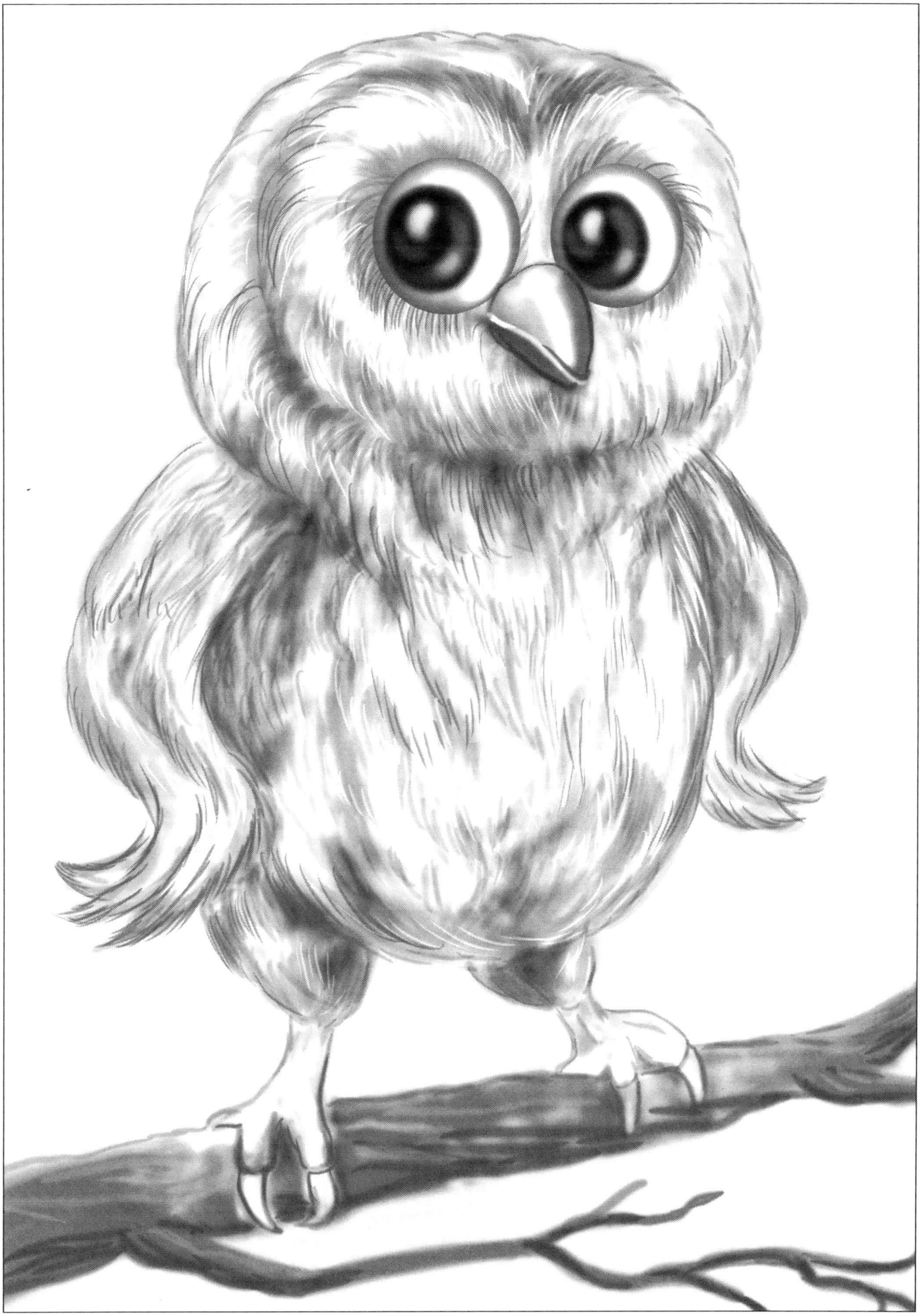

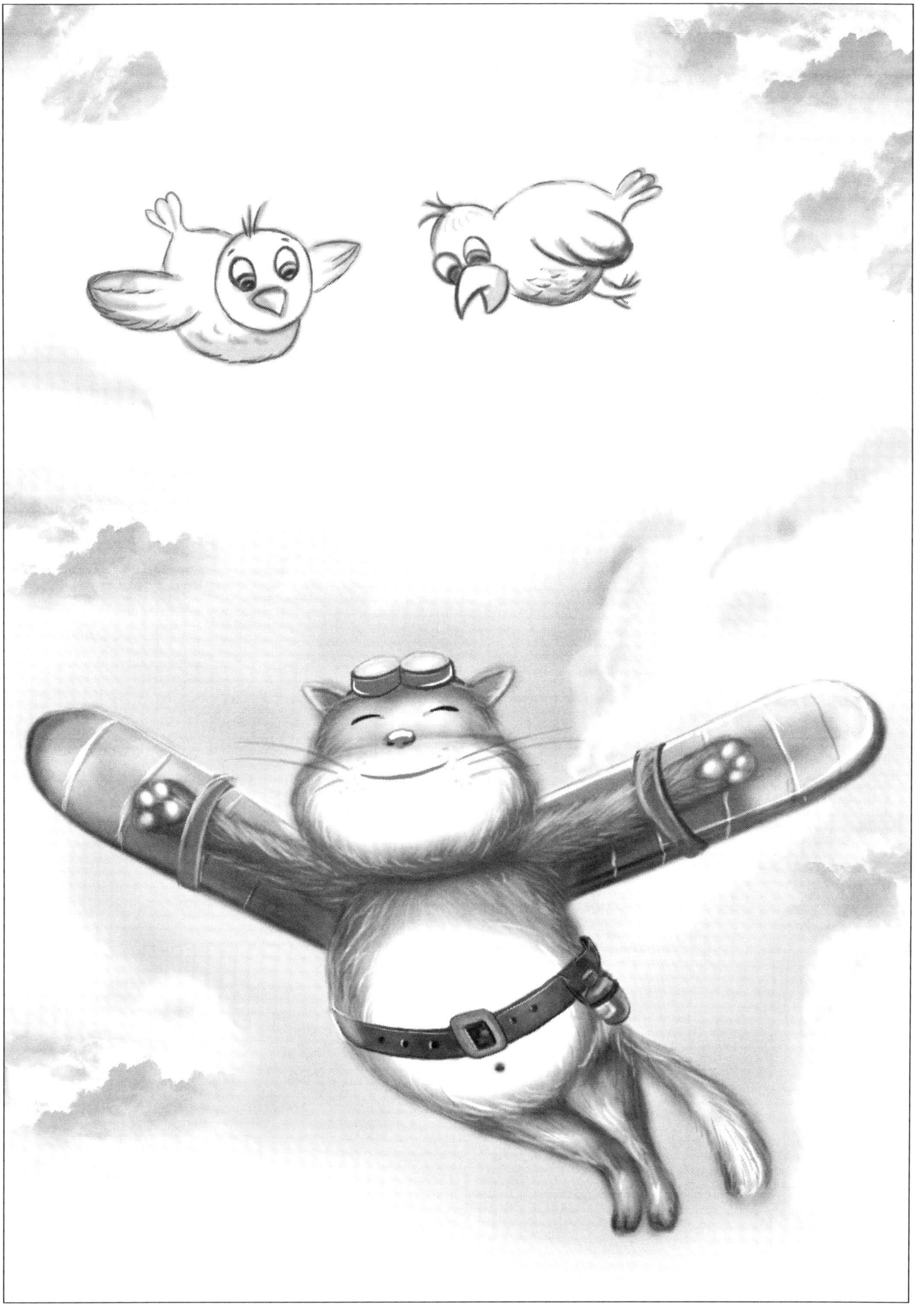

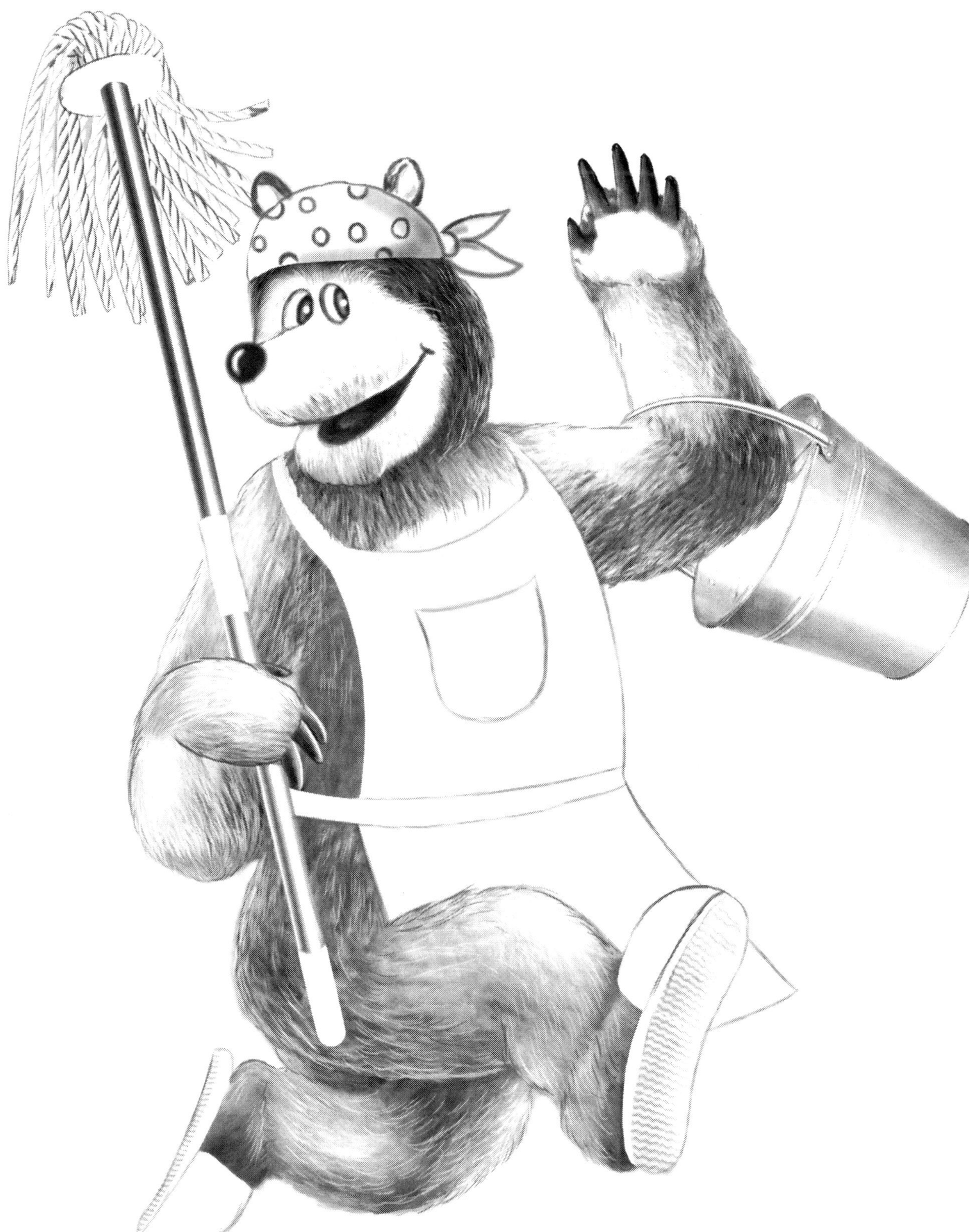

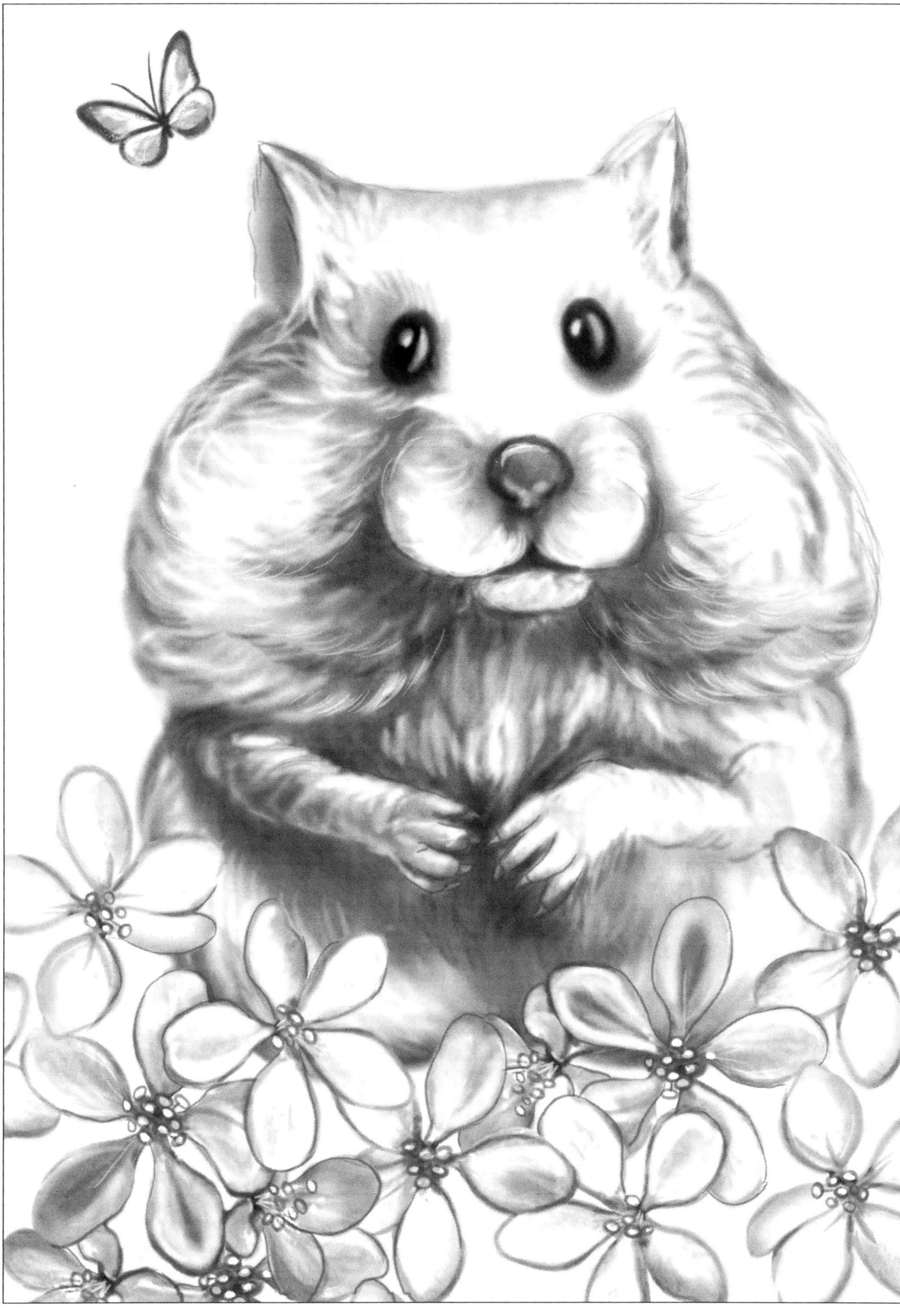

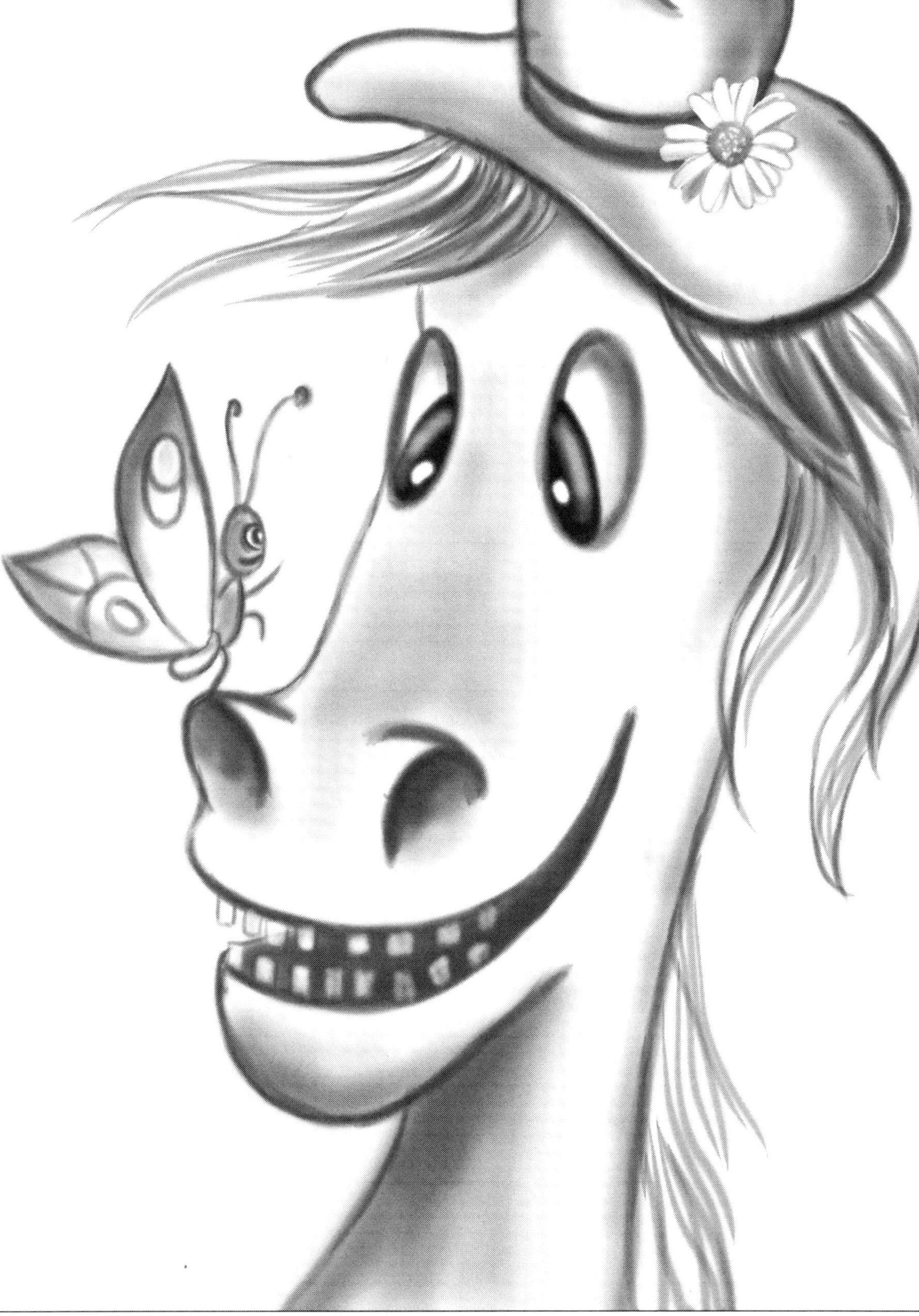

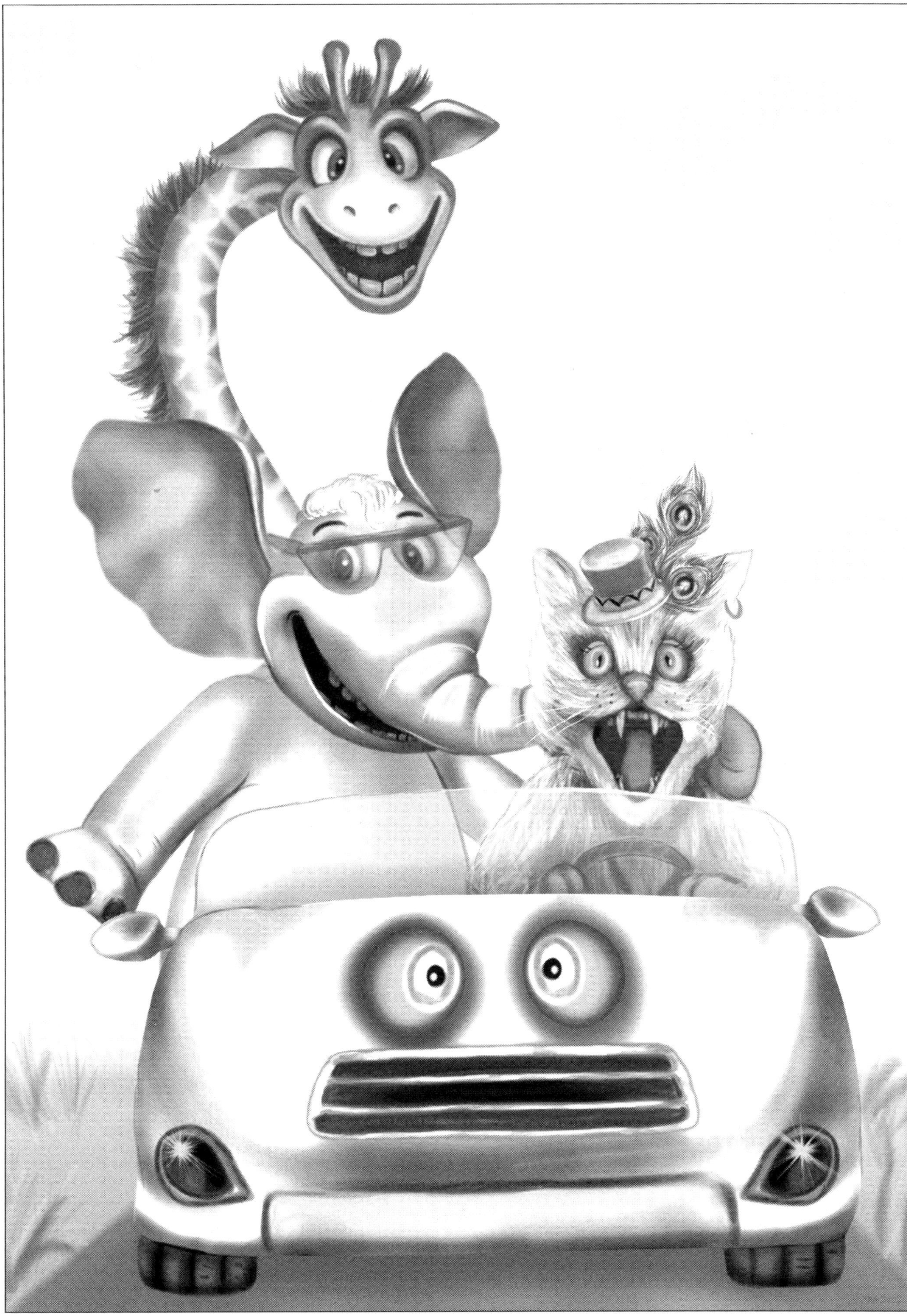

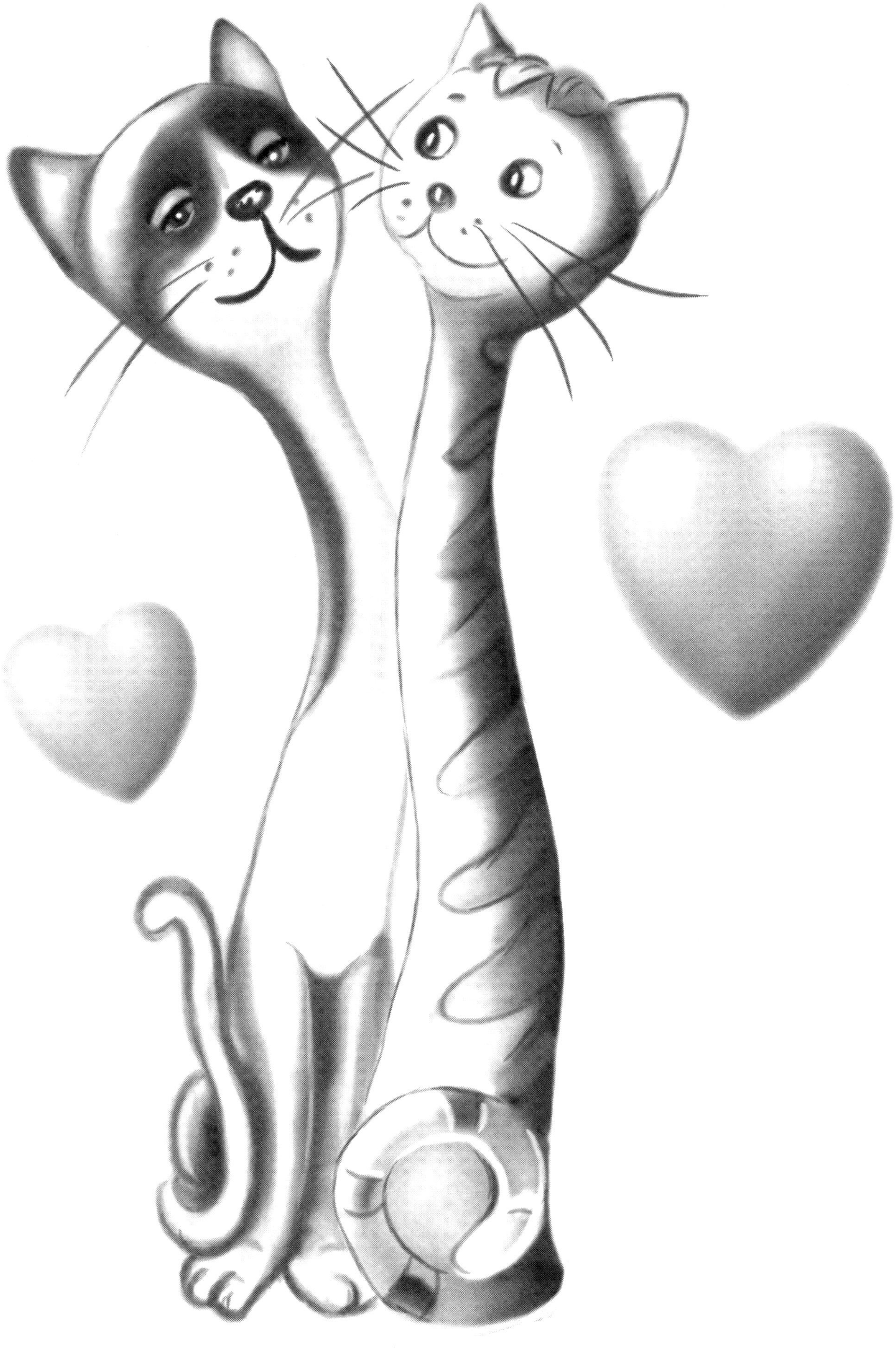

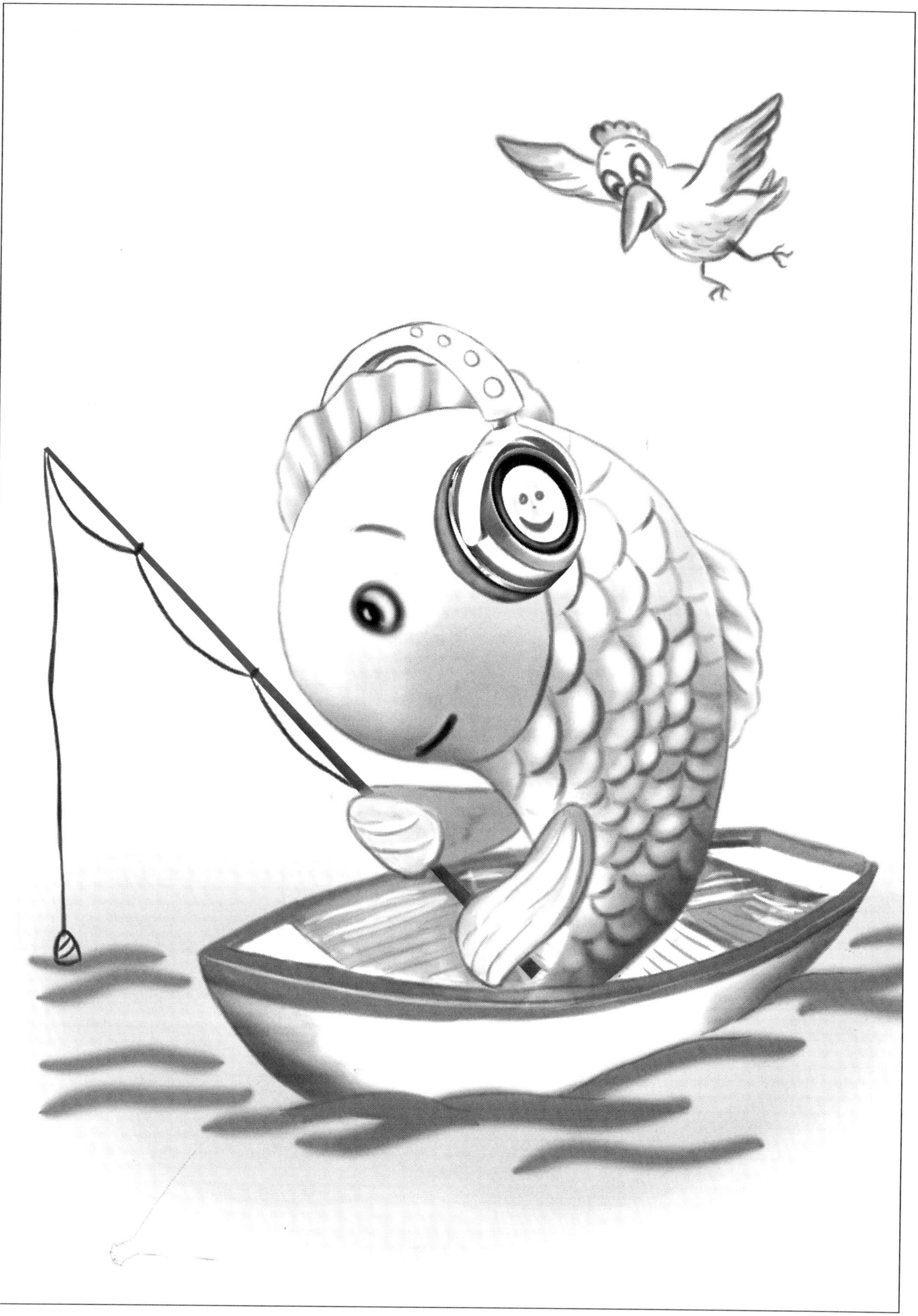

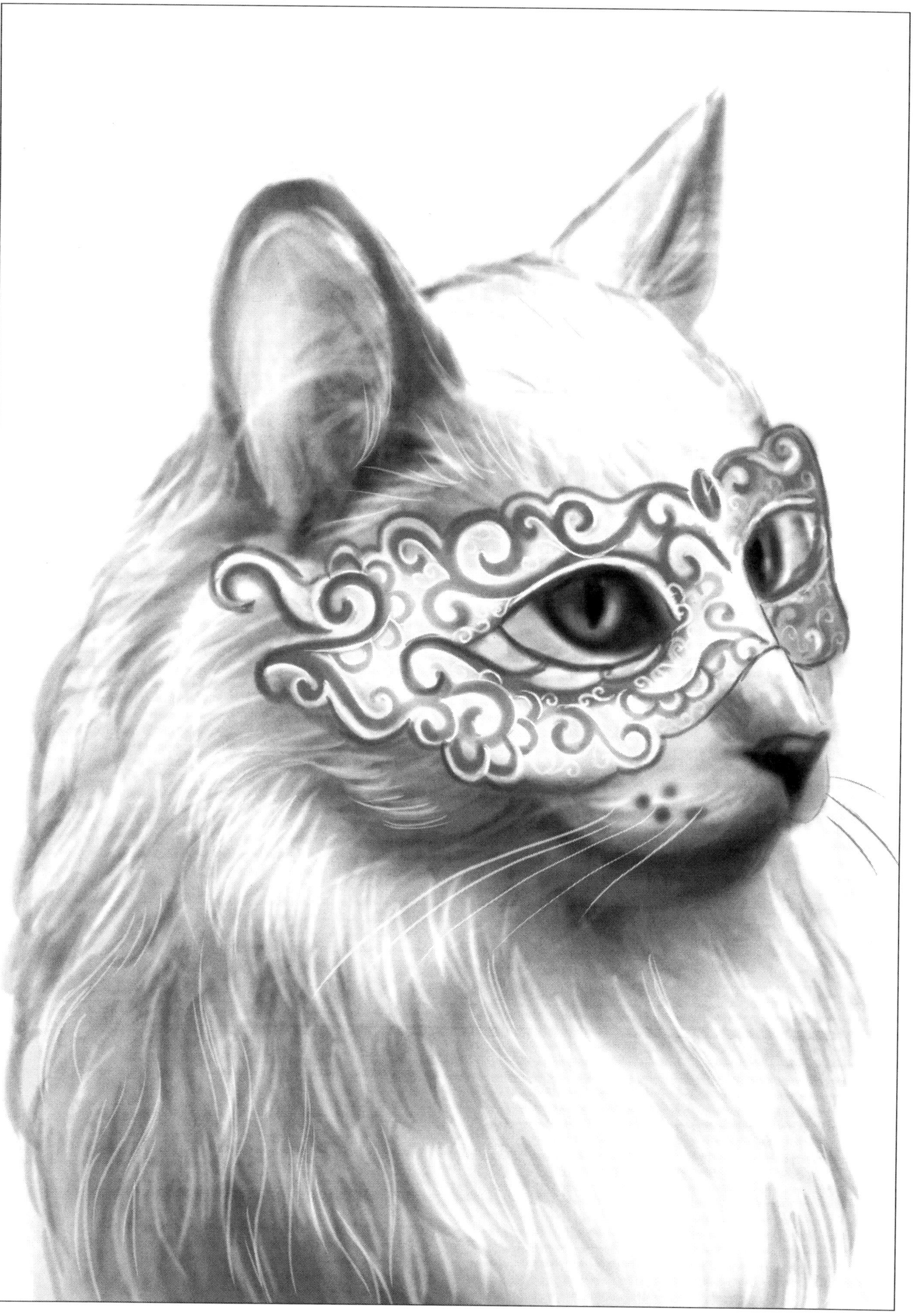

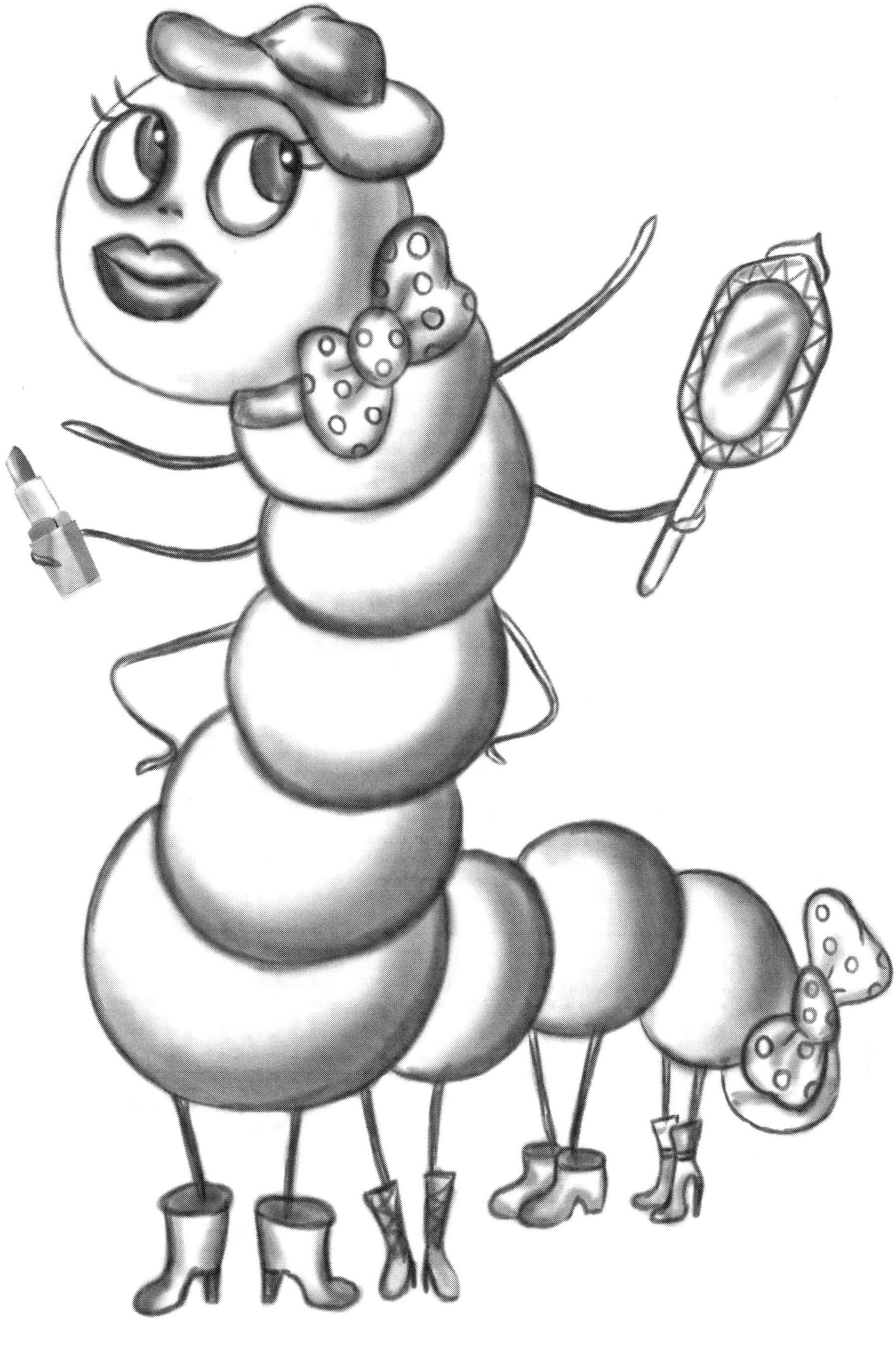

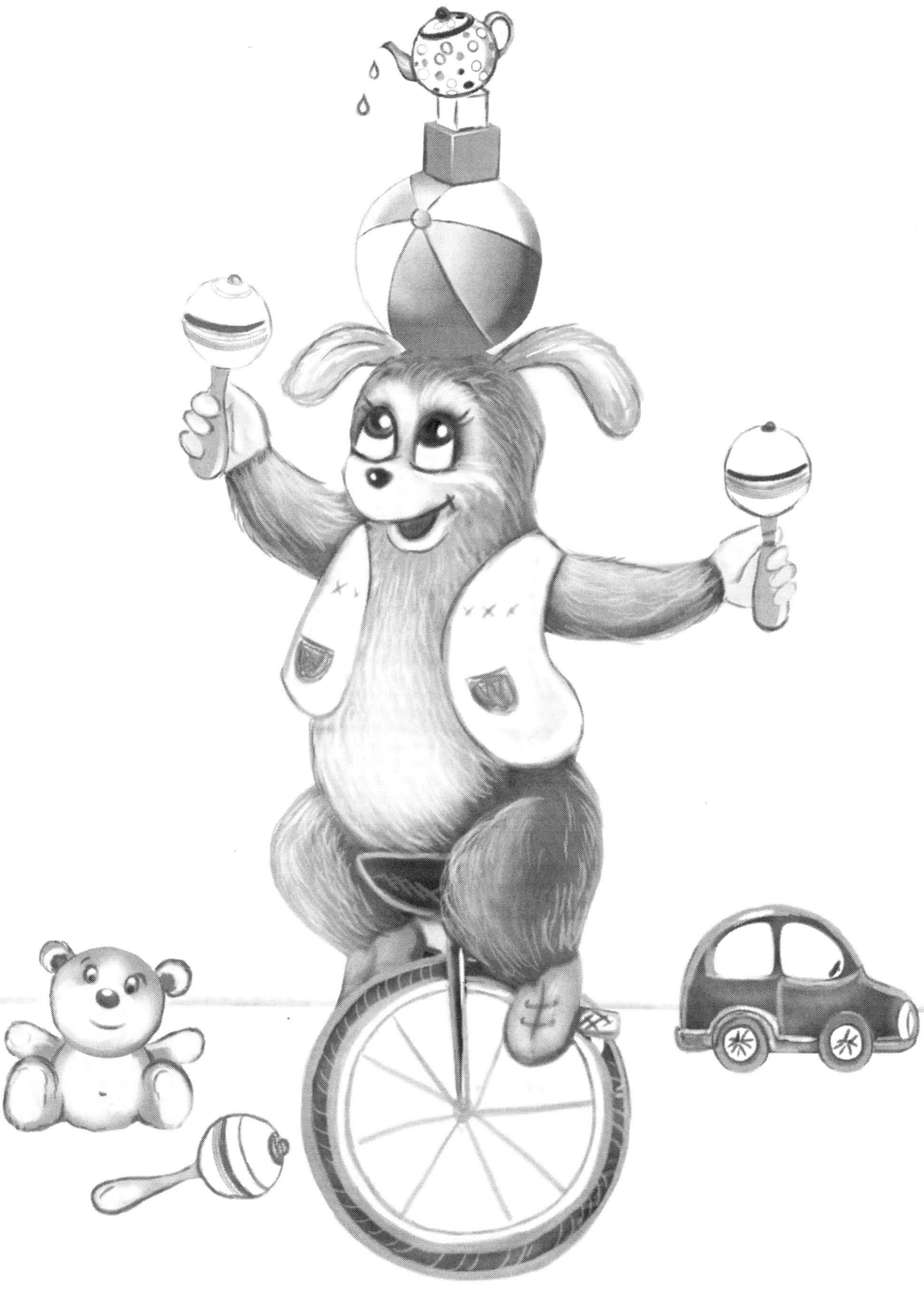

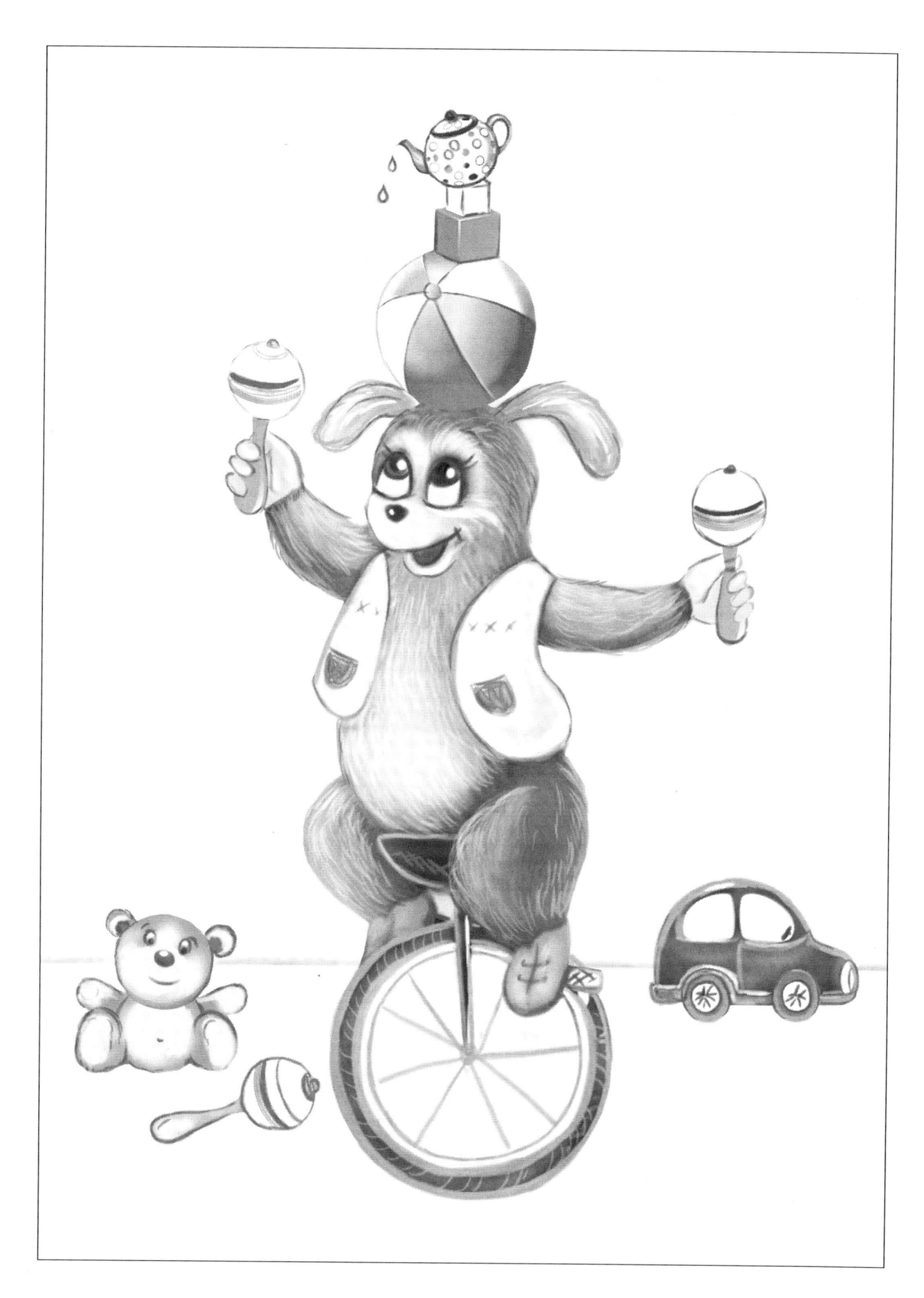

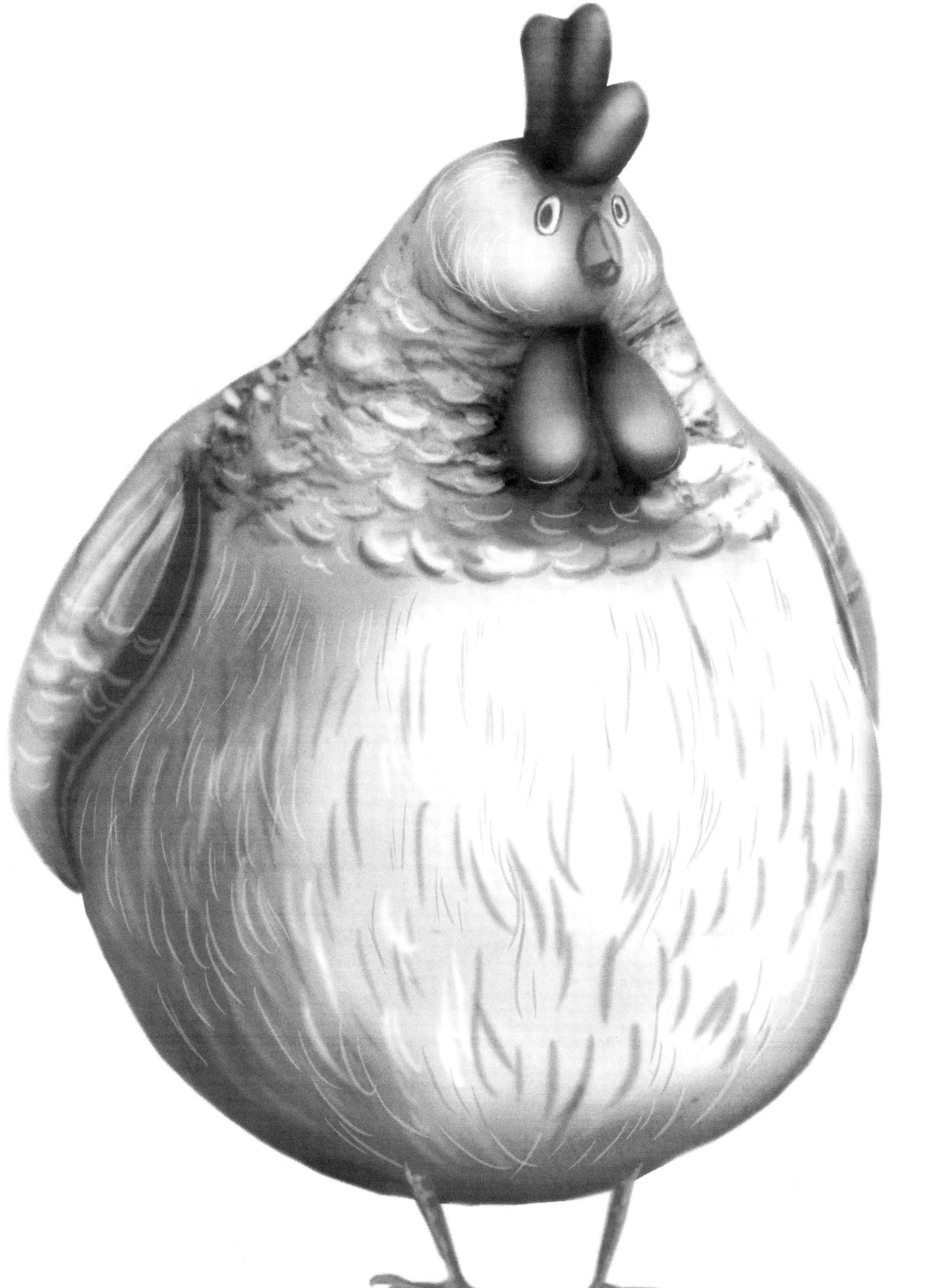

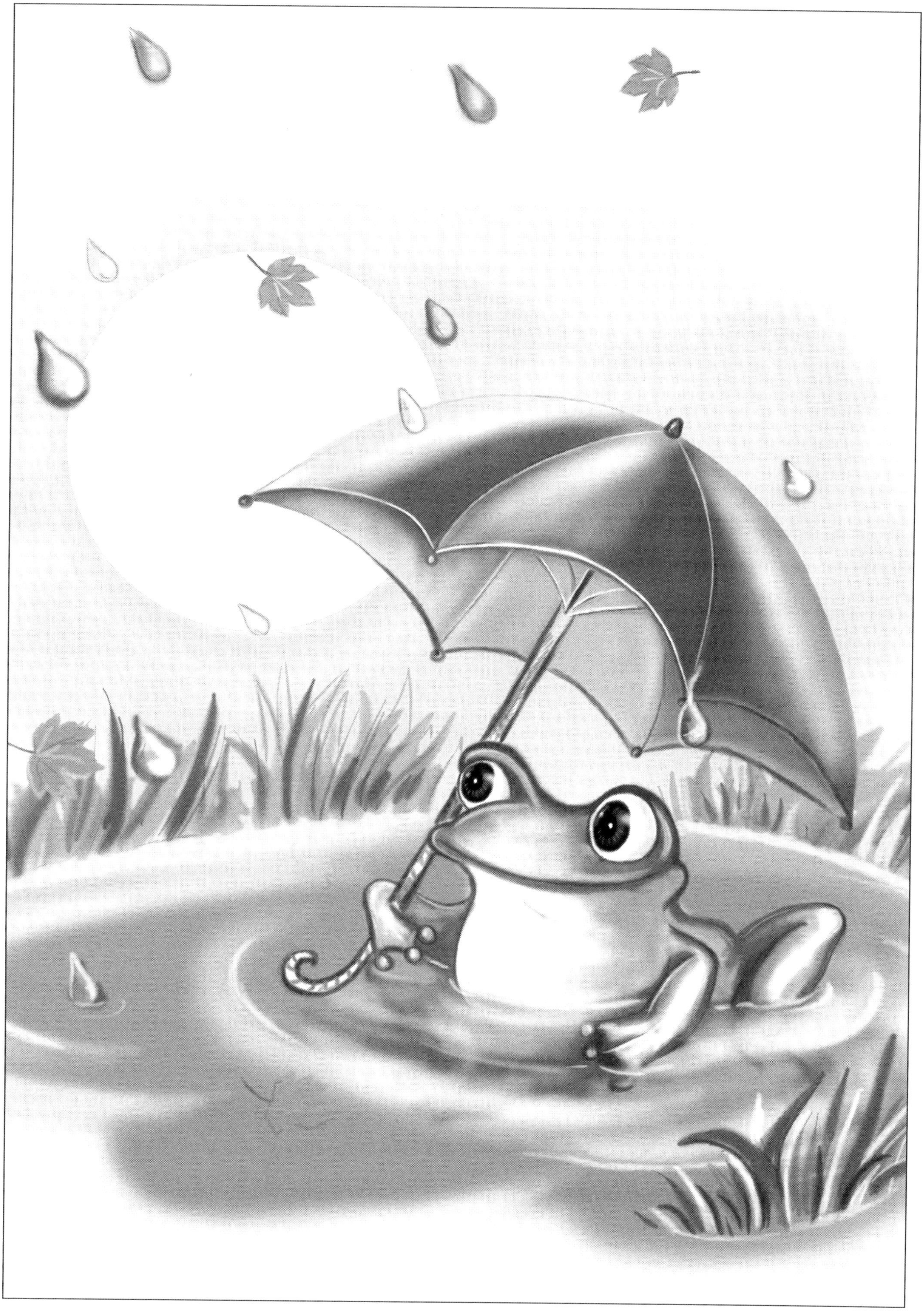

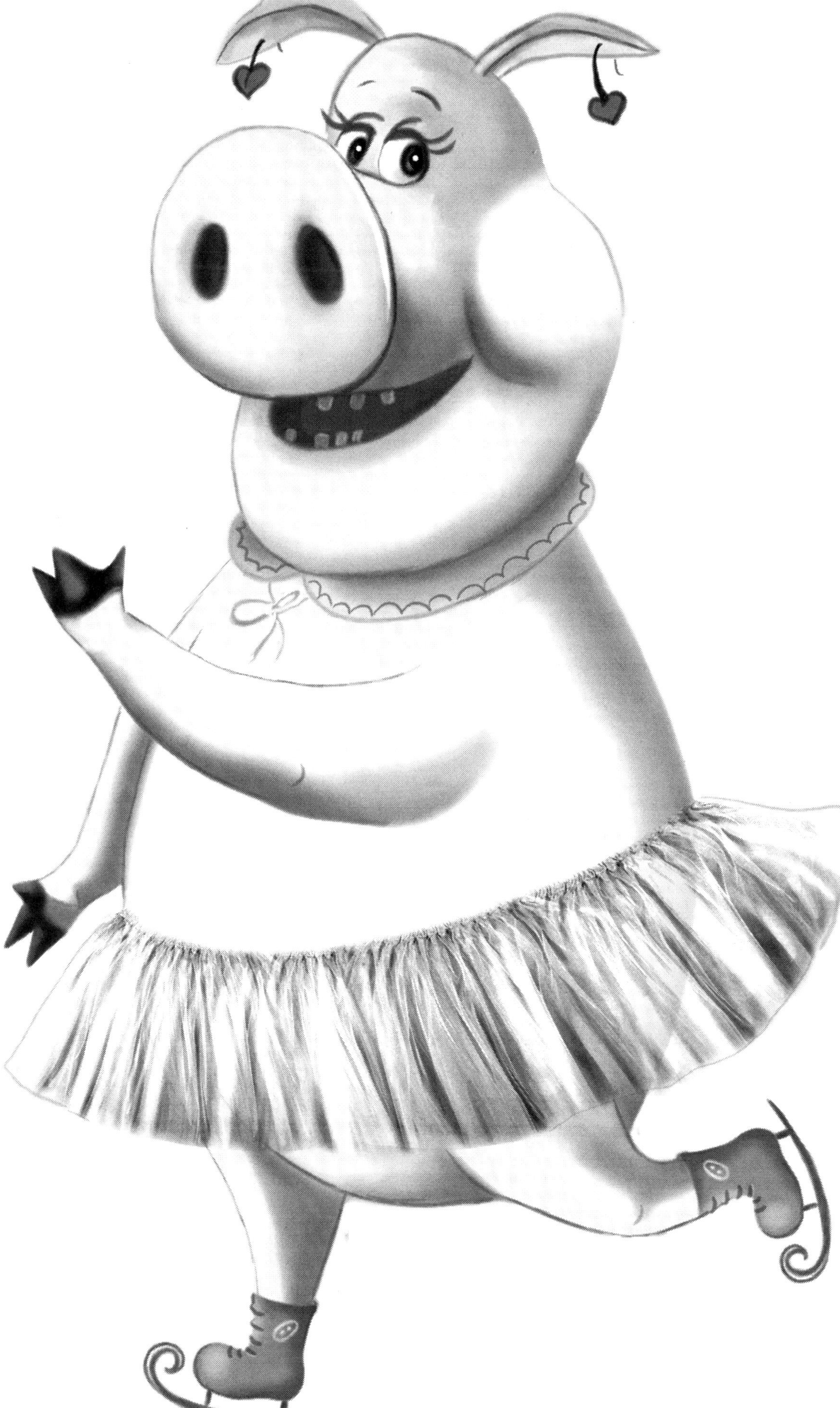

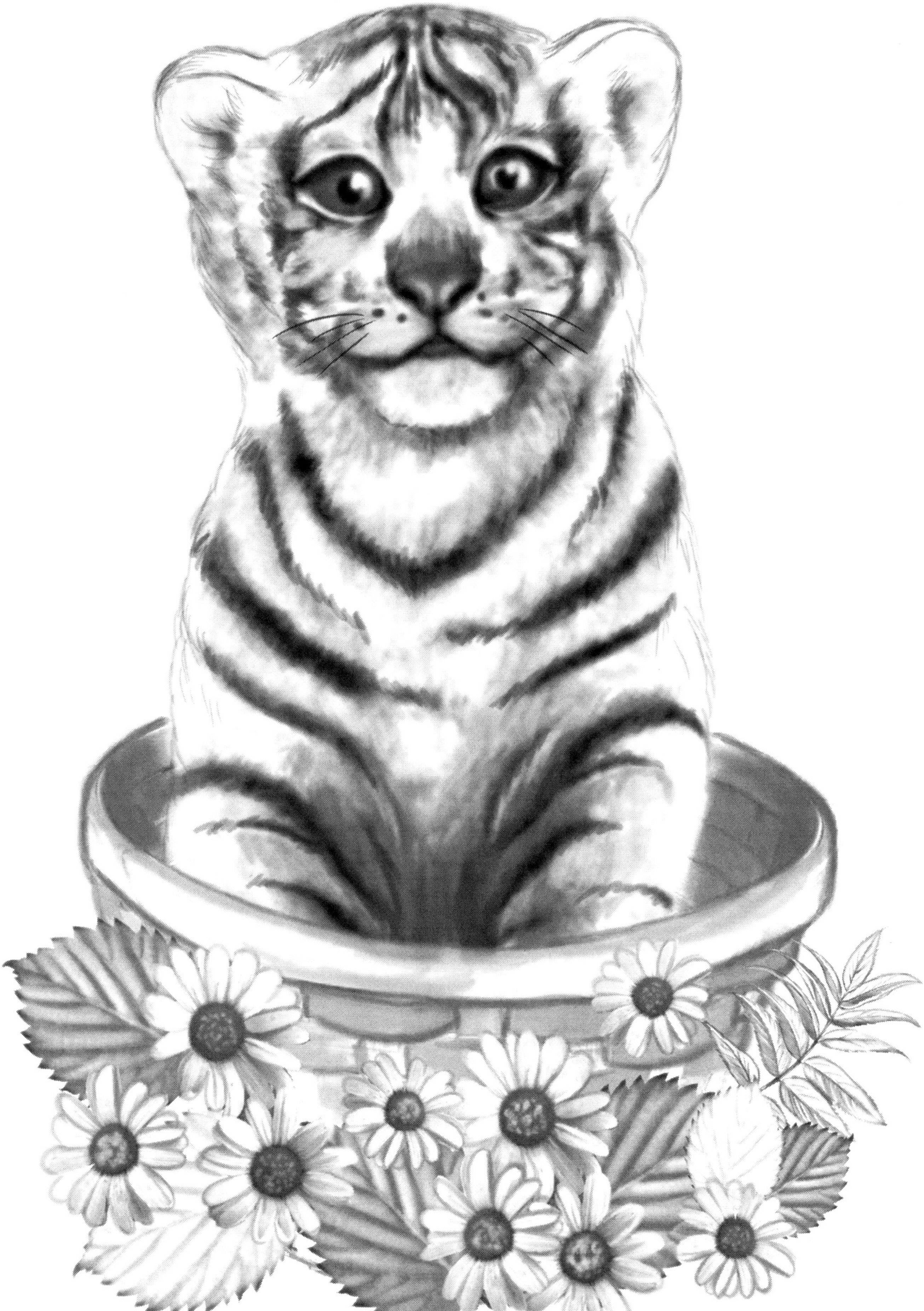

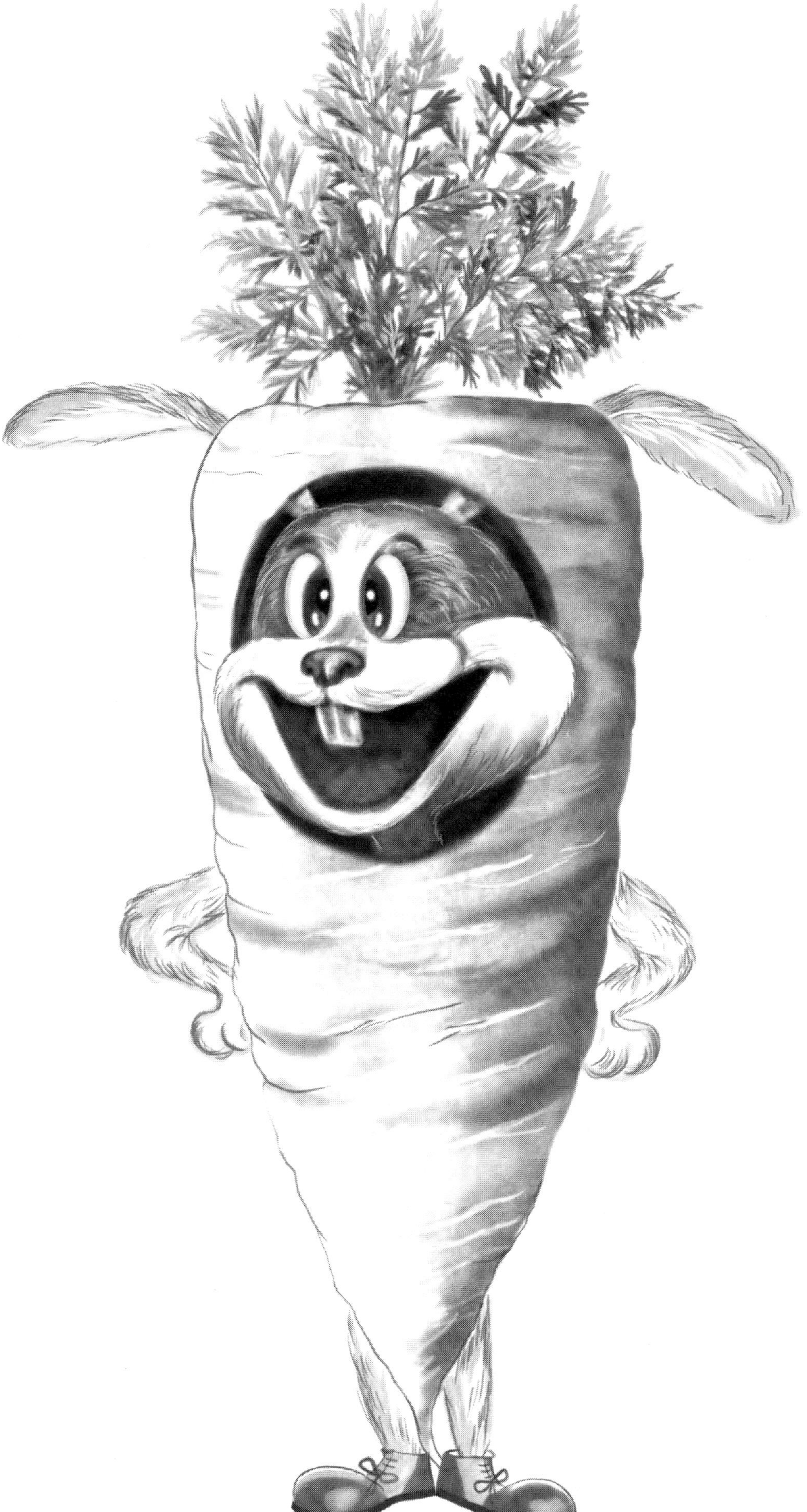

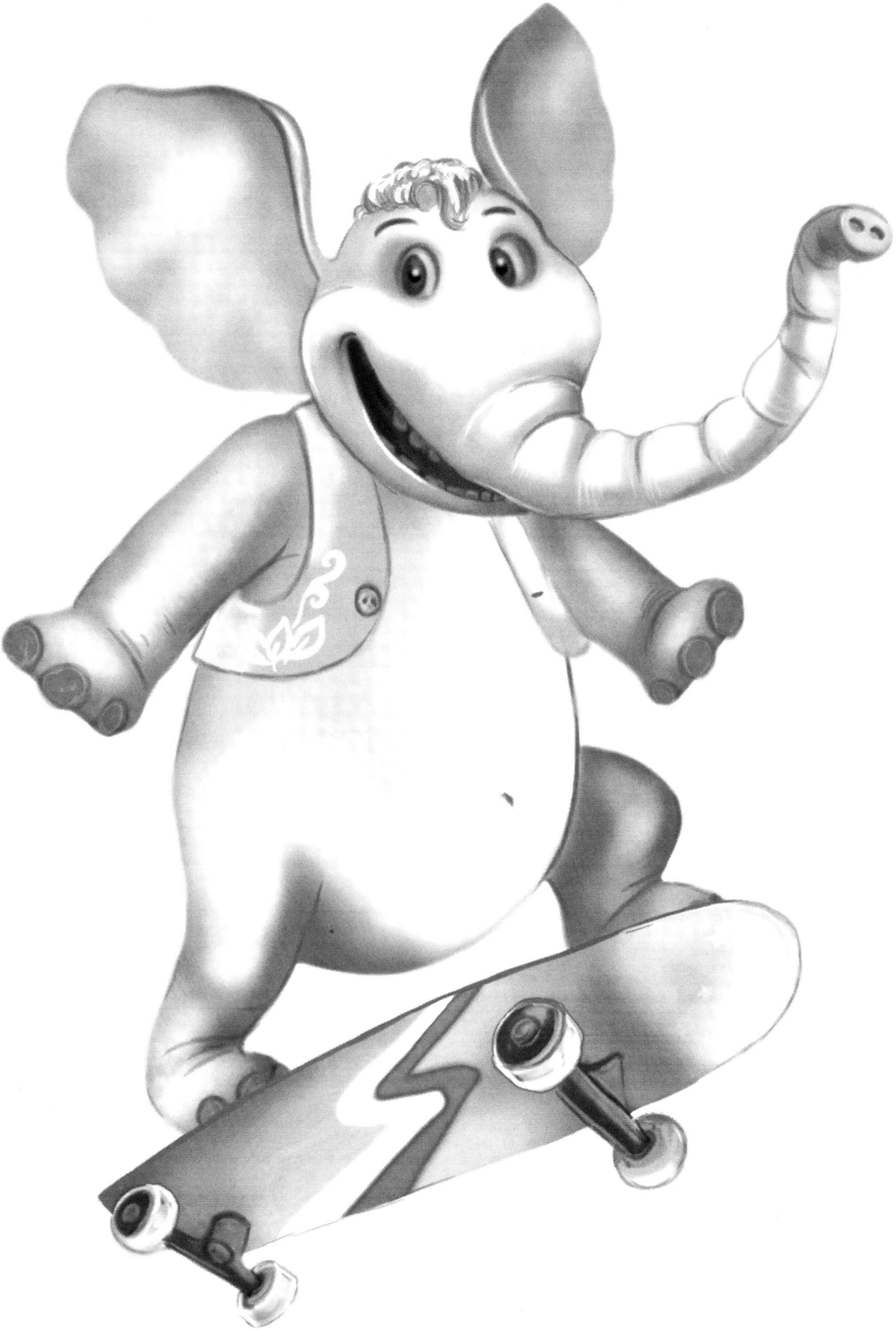

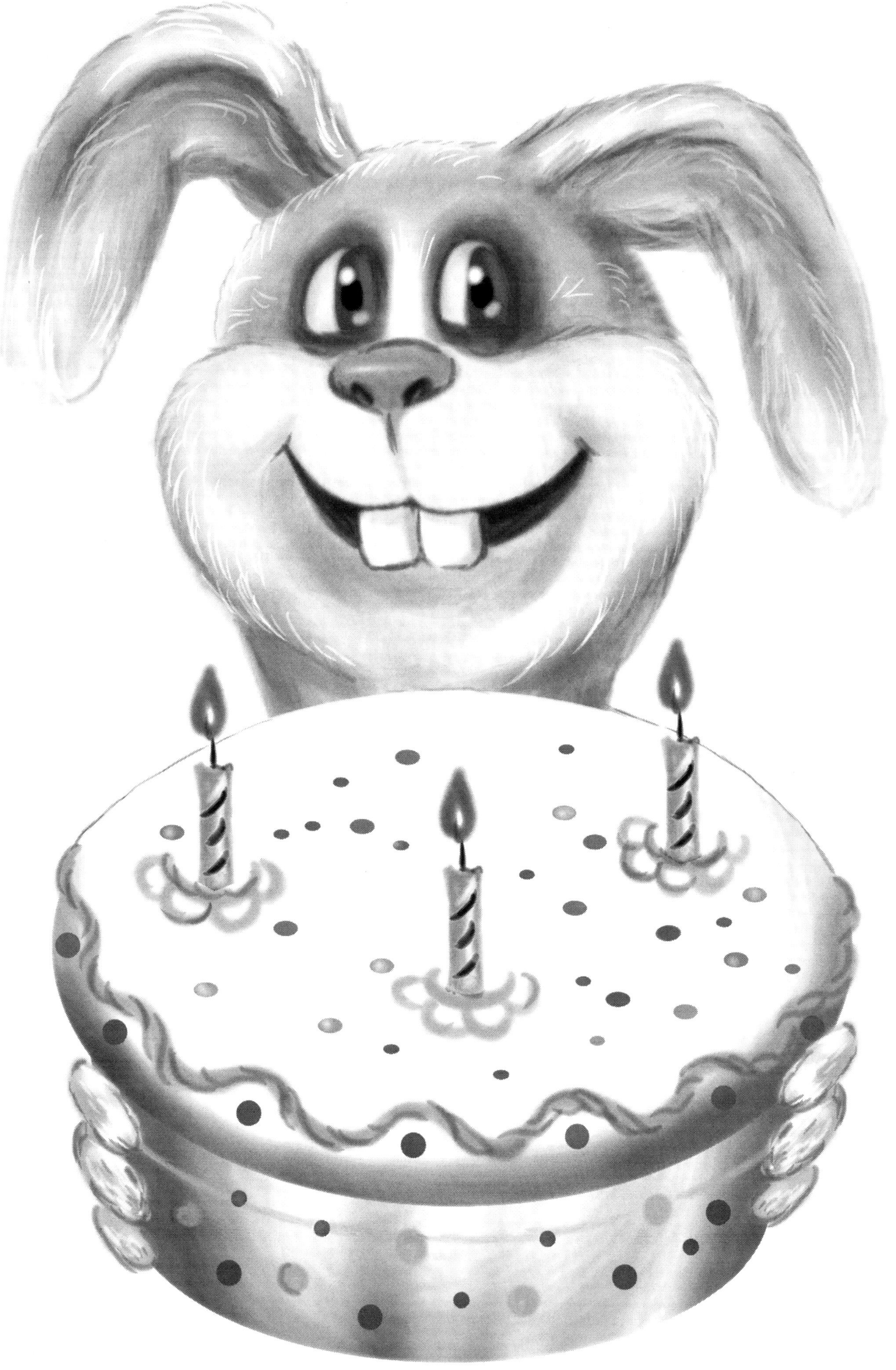

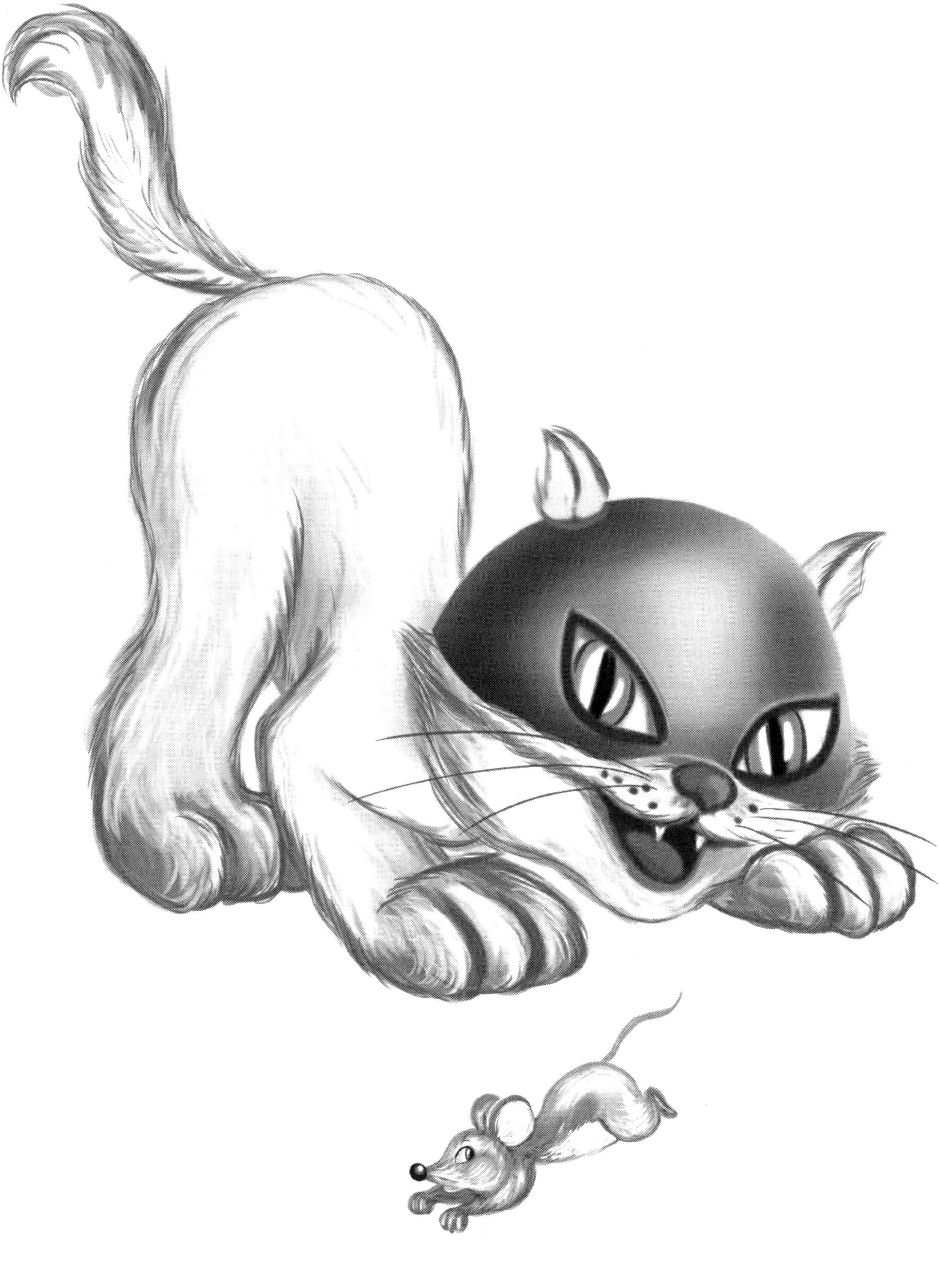

Artist: **Alena Lazareva**

I'm a digital illustrator who mostly works in fantasy style.
I like to represent fairies, angels, mermaids and mystical images.
My artworks are published in magazines of different
countries (England, Australia, Italy, Russia).
My inspirations come for many places. Travel, animals, nature, emotions,
my family, life!
website: **www.alenalazareva.com**

COLORING BOOKS:

Available on Amazon!

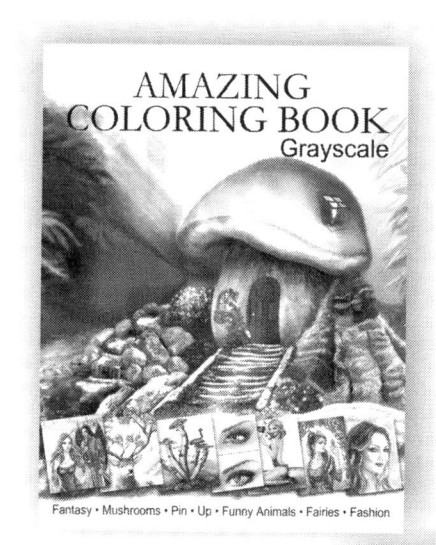

COLORING PAGES:

Please see my printable coloring pages on **Etsy Shop!**

INSTANT DOWNLOAD!

www.etsy.com/shop/FantasyAlenaLazareva

discount of 30%   Use Code: GIFT30

Made in the USA
San Bernardino, CA
13 July 2018